Frankie and Friends Talk Adoption

Pam Kroskie & Marcie Keithley

Contact Information:
PamIndianaAdopteeNetwork@gmail.com
MarcieIndianaAdopteeNetwork@gmail.com

Dedication

For all the Little Peeps

Hi! My name is Frankie, and I'm adopted and hear you are too!

That makes me happy! Would you like us to be friends?

When you're adopted, you may want to ask questions.

It's okay if you want to learn things about the day you were born.

What kind of questions would you like to ask?

When you're adopted, you have another family. I think about my family sometimes.

Do you ever think about your other family?

Can you draw me a picture of what you think your family looks like?

When I look in the mirror, I wonder who I look like.

Do you ever wonder who you look like?

If you do, that's okay!

When it's time to be picked up from school, I worry sometimes and get nervous that my family will forget to pick me up.

Do you ever get nervous or worry?

If you do, that's okay!

Some days I get sad and don't understand why.

Do you get sad sometimes too?

Can you draw me a picture of your sad face?

When it's my birthday, I wonder if my other family is thinking about me too.

Do you think about your other family sometimes on your birthday?

Do you wonder if you have any brothers or sisters?

That's okay!

When I sleep over at my friend's house, all I want to do is go home and be with my family where I feel safe.

Do you ever feel this way when you sleep away from home?

If you feel this way, it's okay to call home.

I wonder why I was adopted.

Do you ever wonder why you were adopted and afraid to ask why?

That's okay!

What would you like to ask about your adoption?

Asking questions is okay, and that's how we learn and grow!

No matter what you are feeling, we are all in this together!

Frankie and friends want you to know that you are amazing just the way you are!

Meet Pam and Marcie

Pam Kroskie and Marcie Keithley are the founders of Indiana Adoptee Network. IAN's focus is on education and the empowerment of feelings common to adoptees of all ages.

Both women are in successful reunions and have been educating families in the adoption community for over ten years. As an adoptee and first mom, they recognize the importance of sharing feelings to build stronger families.

Made in the USA
Middletown, DE
24 October 2021

50935594R00015